This Book Belongs To:

____

BY
Home Planners And
Journals